I SEE YOU

A Faith-Based Guide for Emerging Leaders

DR. SHERRI JOHNSON, RN

Cover and Interior Formatting by KUHN Design Group | kuhndesigngroup.com

I See You: A Faith-Based Leadership Guide for Emerging Leaders
By: Dr. Sherri Johnson, RN

To my parents—Mom and Dad—thank you for shaping me into the woman I am today. Your quiet strength, deep love, and countless sacrifices laid the foundation for who I've become. I am forever grateful and honored to be your daughter.

To Naomi, Imani, Amanda, and Chloe—you each bring light, brilliance, and beauty to this world. May you continue to lead with courage, walk in purpose, and never forget how deeply you are seen and loved.

And to all my nieces, nephews, and mentees—this book is also for you. Your gifts, your perspectives, and your journeys matter deeply. Wherever life takes you, may you rise with confidence, lead with integrity, and always know that your voice belongs. Keep soaring.

And to Tiffany—thank you for your guidance, your sisterhood, and your steady friendship. Your leadership and your heart continue to inspire me, and I'm grateful to walk alongside you in purpose and faith.

CONTENTS

AUTHOR'S NOTE

didn't write this book from a mountaintop. I wrote it from the journey. There was a time when I was just beginning to understand who I was, why I mattered, and how I could lead—even when I felt unsure or unseen. I wrestled with questions: Was I enough? Did I belong? Did I have what it takes?

Now, with more miles behind me and wisdom in my heart, I see that I was always becoming. Every moment—the quiet ones, the hard ones, the brave ones—shaped me into the leader I was meant to be.

This book is my letter to that younger self—and to *you*.

To the emerging leader wondering if your voice matters: it does.

To the quiet one in the back of the room: you are seen.

To the bold dreamer wrestling with fear: you were born for this.

You don't need to have all the answers. You don't need to lead like anyone else. And you certainly don't need to wait for permission to start walking in purpose.

You are becoming. And the world needs *your* kind of leadership.

So let this book be your mirror, your guide, and your reminder: *You were created for this.*

With faith, love, and purpose,
Dr. Sherri

CHAPTER 1

CREATED ON PURPOSE

Owning Your Identity as a Leader

From the moment you were created, your life was imbued with purpose. Even when the world feels noisy or distracted—and even when recognition feels distant—you are never invisible to God.

Your voice matters. Your presence matters. Your story matters.

Leadership isn't about being the loudest in the room; it's about trusting that you were designed to make a difference, even before others take notice. You were created to shine in your own unique way, and every step you take is part of a much bigger plan.

I know this not just from study but from experience.

Growing up in New Jersey, the most densely populated state in the country, I saw early on that opportunities were not evenly distributed. Some neighborhoods boasted great schools, safe parks, and endless resources. Others struggled with fewer options and greater challenges.

I didn't know the term for it back then, but I came to understand it later: the social determinants of health.[1]

---

1. Social determinants of health are the conditions in the places where people live, learn, work, and play that affect their health and quality of life. These include things like access to safe housing, healthy food, good schools, jobs, and healthcare.
   Reference: Centers for Disease Control and Prevention (CDC). (2021, March 10). *Social determinants of health: Know what affects health.*

Even in places where resources were uneven, my parents fought to give us a chance.

My mom balanced a demanding day job with volunteering in the school cafeteria at night, standing for hours during bingo nights to secure a discounted tuition for us. The work wasn't glamorous, and it required that she spend time away from our family. But it was her way of investing in our future.

My dad ran his own accounting firm, teaching me that leadership means taking action without waiting for permission.

Their sacrifices planted seeds I didn't fully understand until later.

But that season showed me this truth: You are created on purpose, for a purpose.

NAVIGATING EXPECTATIONS AND INSECURITY

Being the oldest of three girls in my family came with pressure. Expectations were high at home, in church, and at school. My days were filled with cheerleading, dance, church activities, and helping care for my younger sisters. But even with all that structure, I was navigating an awkward season of *becoming*—growing into who God was calling me to be.

Deep down, I knew I was destined for greater impact. My parents reminded me of this often, and I felt the Holy Spirit whispering it to me, even when I couldn't fully explain it. Still, I moved through a season of uncertainty, learning to trust that my unclear path was shaping me for something greater.

In Catholic school, I was one of the few Black students. I stood out in ways I didn't yet know how to process. I was quiet. Sheltered. Shy. And during those middle school years—when appearance and belonging feel all-consuming—I often felt awkward and overlooked.

That sense of invisibility isn't uncommon. If you've ever felt your presence didn't matter or found yourself shrinking to fit in, you're not alone. Here's what I've learned since:

Your confidence doesn't come from others' affirmation. It comes from knowing *Who* created you—and *why*.

Most importantly, I began to believe God's Word above anyone else's opinion. Jeremiah 1:5 (NKJV) says, "Before I formed you in the womb I knew you…"

That's not just a comforting verse. It's a declaration of your identity, leadership calling, and true purpose.

If you've ever doubted your value, let this be your reminder: You are not here by accident.

You are here to lead.

JOURNAL ACTIVITY: WHO AM I BECOMING?

Reflect on a season in your life when you felt unsure, overlooked, or like you didn't fully fit in.

1. What sustained you during that time—faith, family, or community?

_____

_____

_____

_____

_____

2. In what ways has God been revealing your purpose to you, even in subtle ways?

_____

_____

_____

_____

_____

3. What does it mean to trust God when the path ahead is unclear?

4. How might God be shaping you *right now* for something bigger than you can see?

ACTION PLAN: STEPPING INTO YOUR IDENTITY

1. Affirm Your Identity

Each morning, speak or write three faith-based affirmations. Here are examples you can try:

→ *"I am known by God."*

→ *"I am created with purpose."*

→ *"I am growing into who God designed me to be."*

2. Embrace What Makes You Unique

Write down three things about your background, family, or personality that make you different.

→ These are part of your leadership story—*strengths*, not setbacks.

3. Practice Showing Up

This week, choose one setting (e.g., class, club, or church) where you'll *show up on purpose*. This could mean raising your hand, sharing a new idea, or simply refusing to shrink back.

→ Leadership starts when you stop hiding and start believing that you belong.

REFLECTION

You don't need to have the loudest voice in the room to be a leader. And you don't need a spotlight to make a difference.

God already sees you. And He's already preparing you.

Leadership begins when you start showing up with purpose—using your voice, your presence, and your story, even when it feels uncomfortable.

It's not about being seen by everyone.

It's about being faithful to the calling on your life.

TAKEAWAY

You were created on purpose, for a purpose—and your identity is your leadership foundation.

PRAYER

Lord, thank You for creating me with intention and purpose. Even when I feel unseen, help me to remember that I am fully known and deeply loved by You. Give me the confidence to walk in my identity and the courage to lead with authenticity. Amen.

JOURNAL

CHAPTER 2

RISING THROUGH REJECTION

WHEN BELONGING FEELS OUT OF REACH

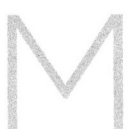iddle school can feel like a relentless test of identity. *Who am I? Where do I belong? Am I enough?*

For me, these questions weren't just internal—they were reinforced by daily interactions. I was still growing into myself, both physically and emotionally. I had a gap between my teeth, acne, and hair that didn't conform to the "standard." I had dreams, ambitions, and curiosity—but none of that seemed to matter when I walked into school and felt instantly out of place.

I made the cheerleading team after failing basketball tryouts. It should've been a win—but instead, it became one of the hardest seasons of my life. As the only dark-skinned girl on the squad, I wasn't just different—I was often treated as less. The cliques, the side-eyes, the locker room comments—they weren't just painful; they were isolating.

If you've ever felt like you were physically present but emotionally excluded, *I see you.*

Sure, the discomfort may be real, but it doesn't define your destiny. It's shaping your strength.

THE COURAGE TO BE DIFFERENT

I never stopped showing up. Not because I felt confident every day, but because something inside me told me that this season was preparing me.

I wasn't the loudest voice. I didn't have the most friends. But I had faith. I had a support system at church, loving parents who spoke truth over me, and a calendar filled with purposeful activities that reminded me of who I was, even when others tried to make me forget.

Eventually, I realized something powerful: Their rejection wasn't a reflection of my worth—it was a reflection of their own limitations.

"You were made for greater things," my parents always told me. And I began to believe it, even when the world around me didn't.

REJECTION IS NOT THE END

One day in the locker room, I asked to borrow a classmate's hairspray. Before she could respond, one of the "mean girls" made a loud, cutting joke about my hair. The room erupted with laughter. But I didn't cry. I didn't lash out. I held onto my dignity and walked out with my head high.

That moment—and countless others like it—taught me what leadership truly means.

It's not about popularity or titles; it's about strength of character.

I began to realize that when you choose to stand tall after someone tries to tear you down, you discover what real leadership looks like. It's choosing dignity over drama and courage over comfort.

JOURNAL ACTIVITY: YOUR STRENGTH STORY

Write about a time you felt rejected, excluded, or underestimated.

- How did it feel in that moment?

- What did this experience teach you about your strength, empathy, or courage?

- How has it shaped the kind of leader you want to become?

ACTION PLAN: BUILDING INNER CONFIDENCE

1. Speak Truth over yourself.

Find a Bible verse that affirms your worth. Not sure where to start? Try Jeremiah 1:5 (NKJV) "Before I formed you in the womb I knew you" or Psalm 139:14 (NKJV) "I am fearfully and wonderfully made." Write it down and place it somewhere visible—your mirror, phone, or journal.

2. Reframe rejection.

Recall a time someone excluded, judged, or belittled you. Ask yourself: *Was that about me, or about them?* Write one sentence that affirms your value, regardless of how others treat you.

3. Be someone's ally.

Leadership means lifting others up. Look for someone who might feel left out at school, work, or church. Choose to sit with them, speak up for them, or show kindness. Small actions create real impact.

REFLECTION

Rejection doesn't define your worth—it reveals your strength. Some of the most powerful leaders are those who've walked through painful moments and still choose kindness, purpose, and grace.

TAKEAWAY

You don't need everyone's approval to walk in your calling. God chose you, and that's enough.

PRAYER

Father, thank You for seeing me fully, even when others overlook me. When I feel rejected or unseen, remind me that I am chosen, called, and deeply loved by You. Strengthen me to rise with confidence and lead with compassion, even in the hard moments. Amen.

JOURNAL

CHAPTER 3

DISCOVERING DIRECTION THROUGH PURPOSE

LEADERSHIP STARTS WITH SMALL STEPS

High school is often painted as a time of uncertainty—but it's also a season of discovery. The pressure to fit in, excel, and "figure it all out" can be overwhelming. But what if leadership isn't about having a five-year plan? What if it's about showing up in the everyday, right where you are?

You don't need a title to lead. You just need a willingness to serve, speak up, and stay grounded in your values.

For me, leadership began in small moments: joining school clubs, teaching Sunday school, joining the cheerleading team, co-founding a dance group, volunteering at the hospital, and speaking on a panel about "Cultural Tolerance."[2] These moments may not have seemed monumental at the time—but each one was a step toward purpose.

Looking back, I see how it started. And maybe, you're already becoming a leader too—you just may not have realized it yet.

---

2. In the past, the term *cultural tolerance* was often used to describe how we relate to people from different backgrounds. But "tolerance" implies simply putting up with someone—without true understanding or respect. Over time, that language has evolved into more thoughtful concepts like *cultural humility*. Cultural humility means being open to learning from others, reflecting on our own biases, and leading with empathy and respect. It's not about having all the answers—it's about being willing to listen, learn, and grow.

NOTICING THE SPARK

One moment changed everything for me. During a hospital field trip with my school's Medical Explorers Club, I shadowed a perioperative nurse. I stood in the operating room, observing a surgical procedure. But what caught my attention wasn't the tools or the doctors—it was the nurse.

The way she cared for the patient. Her calm confidence. Her ability to connect.

That moment lit a spark in me. I wanted to be *that*—a steady presence, a difference-maker.

God often reveals your calling through everyday experiences. You just need to pay attention.

WHEN COMMUNITY SHAPES YOU

In high school, I wasn't just shaped by the clubs and activities I joined—I was shaped by the people who invested in me. My church community reminded me of my identity. My civic engagement club challenged me to lead with integrity. And my parents? They were my anchor.

I still remember the letter my mom wrote during my Peer Leadership retreat. It simply said, "You were destined for greatness." I've kept that letter, tucked in my Bible to this day.

Leadership is forged in moments like these—when someone sees your potential before you fully do. But I've also learned another truth: even if no one has said those words to you yet, they are no less true. So if no one has spoken life over you, let me say it now: *You are capable. You are called. And you were created for impact.*

No, you don't need a large network or a perfect family to become a leader. Sometimes, leadership starts in quiet moments—when you notice what makes you come alive and take a step toward cultivating that potential.

So whether you have a cheering squad or are still building your circle, know this: **God sees what's in you, and He's already preparing you.**

JOURNAL ACTIVITY: LOOKING FOR CLUES

List three activities or moments in high school (or recently) that made you feel **energized**, proud, or purposeful. What do they reveal about your strengths, passions, or leadership style?

ACTION PLAN: WALKING IN PURPOSE

1. Explore Your Interests

Join a club, attend a workshop, or shadow someone whose work inspires you. Let curiosity lead you toward purpose.

2. Ask Others What They See in You

Sometimes, mentors or friends notice strengths we miss. Ask two people:

- "What's one leadership strength you see in me?"

3. Serve with Intention

This month, find one way to give back—at school, church, or in your community—in a space that aligns with your values.

REFLECTION

Purpose often whispers before it shouts. It might appear in a class that excites you, a moment you felt useful, or a compliment that stuck with you. Don't ignore those clues. They're breadcrumbs guiding you toward something greater.

TAKEAWAY

You don't need to have it all figured out right now. Just keep saying yes to the next right opportunity.

PRAYER

Lord, thank You for placing purpose inside of me. Open my eyes to the opportunities You've given me to lead and serve. Help me walk confidently toward this calling, even when the road ahead feels uncertain. Amen.

JOURNAL

CHAPTER 4

TURNING ADVERSITY INTO STRENGTH

PAIN WITH A PURPOSE

f you've ever faced something that felt unfair, overwhelming, or just plain hard, you're not alone. Many of us carry silent battles—bullying, family stress, self-doubt, or grief—and we wonder, *Will this always define me?*

The truth? It doesn't have to.

Sometimes our greatest pain lays the foundation for our deepest strength.

In middle and high school, I endured ridicule, exclusion, and disappointment. At the time, I didn't see how God was working, but those challenges were building something within me that couldn't be shaken—compassion, conviction, and spiritual strength that would later prepare me to lead with empathy and integrity.

THE PAGEANT THAT REMINDED ME

One defining moment came during the Miss American Pre-Teen Pageant. After mustering up the courage to ask my parents to let me compete—and preparing as though my future depended on it—I placed in the top twenty out of 300 contestants.

No, I didn't win a crown. But I won something far more meaningful: the reminder that I could show up, take risks, and shine—*without* changing who I was.

That experience gave me a glimpse of what leadership would eventually require: confidence in my identity, even when others don't fully see or understand me.

WHEN FAITH FILLS THE GAPS

Don't get me wrong—days still came when I felt invisible. But in those quiet moments, I leaned into my faith. Scripture reminded me that I was seen and known by God, that I wasn't walking alone, and that my future rested in His hands, not in a crowd (or lack thereof).

If you've ever felt unseen, hear this:

You are not invisible to the One who created you. Nothing you've been through is wasted. God can transform every challenge, heartbreak, and every setback into building blocks for the purpose He's placed on your life.

JOURNAL ACTIVITY:
LOOKING BACK, RISING STRONG

1. Reflect on a time when you faced a difficult situation—rejection, loss, or disappointment. What emotions did you experience? What felt hardest to bear?

2. Now view that moment through a different lens. What did you learn about yourself? How did it deepen your compassion, courage, or faith?

3. Write one truth to hold onto the next time life feels heavy.

_____

_____

_____

_____

_____

_____

_____

ACTION PLAN:
TURNING STRUGGLES INTO STRENGTH

1. Name a Lesson from a Hard Season:

Reflect on a past challenge and identify one positive trait it helped you develop, such as courage, empathy, or determination. Write it down.

2. Find Strength in Scripture:

Choose a verse that reminds you God is with you in struggles (e.g., Isaiah 41:10 or Romans 8:28). Write it somewhere visible so you can read it whenever you need encouragement.

3. Encourage Someone Else:

This week, reach out to someone who might be struggling. Offer a kind word, a listening ear, or a prayer. Healing often flows both ways.

REFLECTION

Some of the strongest leaders are shaped in quiet, hidden places and seasons. You don't need to pretend to have it all together—God performs powerful work in moments of struggle. Your pain doesn't disqualify you; it *prepares* you.

JOURNAL

CHAPTER 5

MAPPING YOUR FUTURE

Planning with Purpose

YOUR LIFE IS NOT ON PAUSE

Maybe you've heard someone say, "You've got time." And while that might be true, it doesn't mean you should wait to begin. Leadership doesn't start when you graduate, land the job, or gain a title—it starts the moment you decide to live on purpose.

Even if you don't have all the answers, now is the perfect season to reflect on what excites you, what burdens your heart, and what feels like a calling. Purpose reveals itself when you start paying attention.

DISCOVERING WHAT MOVES YOU

Looking back, I see how volunteering at a hospital, joining a medical club, and mentoring younger students weren't just extracurricular activities—they were bread-crumbs leading me toward my calling.

You may not have a clear path yet, and that's okay. But when you consider what brings you joy, what challenges stir your heart, and where you naturally lead or serve, you'll start to notice the clues.

Ask yourself:

- What would I do even if I weren't paid for it?

- What issues or causes do I care deeply about?

- When do I feel most alive?

God often places our purpose at the intersection of your passion and compassion.

GOD INVITES YOU INTO THE PLANNING

We sometimes forget that God cares about our goals and dreams. But He does. He wants to walk with you as you explore your gifts, set intentions, and make plans. Leadership is a series of intentional decisions—fueled by faith, guided by wisdom, and rooted in purpose.

Whether you aspire to be a nurse, teacher, entrepreneur, or advocate, you don't need to have it all figured out. Simply ask: "Lord, what's the next step?"

JOURNAL ACTIVITY:
CLARIFYING YOUR CALLING

1. List three things you genuinely enjoy doing—activities that come naturally or bring you joy.

2. List three issues or needs in the world that move your heart.

3. Look for overlap. What careers or roles bridge your joys and concerns?

4. Invite God into the process: Write a prayer asking Him to reveal more of your purpose.

ACTION PLAN: SETTING SPIRIT-LED GOALS

1. Set one short-term goal you can achieve in the next six months

(e.g., enroll in a class, apply for a program, or join a group).

2. Set one long-term goal for the next five to ten years

(e.g., earning a degree, pursuing a career, or serving).

3. Schedule a check-in

Set a monthly reminder to revisit your goals, reflect on your progress, and pray over them.

REFLECTION

You don't need to have everything figured out to walk in purpose. You just need faith for the next step—and the courage to take it.

TAKEAWAY

Purpose is not a destination—it's a daily choice to live intentionally, trust God's timing, and keep moving forward.

PRAYER

Father, thank You for creating me with purpose. Help me hear Your voice and witness Your guidance as I plan my future. Grant me clarity, courage, and peace as I step into the path You've prepared for me. Amen.

JOURNAL

CHAPTER 6

BECOMING THROUGH FAITH AND BELONGING

FROM UNCERTAINTY TO UNSHAKABLE CONFIDENCE

College can feel like stepping into a whole new world—exciting, uncertain, and brimming with possibility. I chose Hampton University, an HBCU steeped in legacy and pride, because I knew I could thrive in its vibrant culture. As someone who loves to learn, the culture resonated with me. Still, I arrived with a mix of nerves and hope, unsure of what lay ahead.

That was when the shift began. Growth takes root in environments that nurture your purpose, even before you fully recognize it. At Hampton, professors didn't just teach—they mentored. My classmates became family. Over time, I realized I wasn't just earning a degree—I was becoming the leader God had been shaping me to be all along.

FINDING STRENGTH IN COMMUNITY

I didn't navigate nursing school alone. I found my "tribe"—friends who prayed with me, studied alongside me, encouraged me when I felt overwhelmed, and held me accountable to my goals. We celebrated each other's victories and supported one another through setbacks. **That circle shaped me.**

Leadership is not a solo journey. The people you surround yourself with will either stretch you or hold you back. Choose those who inspire you to become the best version of yourself. **Ask yourself:** *Who helps me grow into my fullest potential?*

Belonging doesn't mean losing your individuality. It means discovering your strength through a community that reminds you of your identity, redirects you to your purpose during tough times, and celebrates your growth.

TAKING RISKS AND TRUSTING GOD'S TIMING

College brought real challenges: academic rigor, financial stress, personal loss, and moments of public disappointment. I competed in pageants. I worked while balancing a full course load. I grieved loved ones. And yet I kept going.

Each setback became a classroom of its own, teaching me how to rise, reflect, grow, and trust God's timing when my plans faltered.

Leadership isn't always about holding a microphone or wearing a title. Sometimes, it's the quiet resolve to stay in the race, even when quitting feels easier.

JOURNAL ACTIVITY:
WHERE ARE YOU GROWING?

1. Stretch Zone:

What aspect of your life is pushing you to grow right now—school, work, relationships, or faith? Describe how it's stretching you.

_____

_____

_____

_____

_____

2. Your People:

Who helps you stay grounded and motivated? Who cheers you on when things feel tough?

_____

_____

_____

_____

_____

3. Purpose in the Present:

Is there something in your current season that might be preparing you for what's next, even if it's not yet clear?

_____

_____

_____

_____

_____

ACTION PLAN: CREATING
YOUR GROWTH ENVIRONMENT

1. Check Your Circle:

List three people you spend the most time with. Do they inspire growth, positivity, or purpose? If not, identify someone you'd like to connect with and reach out.

2. Find a Mentor:

Think of a teacher, advisor, coach, or community member you admire. Introduce yourself or schedule a time to learn about their journey. Growth accelerates when you learn from others.

3. Pause and Reflect:

Choose one day each week to check in with yourself. What are you learning? What's working? Where do you need support? Use this time to pray, journal, or simply breathe.

REFLECTION

Leadership isn't confined to a classroom, title, or degree. It's shaped through experiences, relationships, and how you show up in everyday life. Whether you're learning in college, on the job, through service, or in your community, **leadership emerges in both formal and informal spaces.** Let God use your current season to stretch, strengthen, and prepare you for what's next.

TAKEAWAY

Growth happens wherever you're planted. Surround yourself with people who believe in you and challenge you, you'll grow into the leader God created you to be.

PRAYER

God, thank You for the people and places shaping me. Keep me rooted in faith, open to learning, and courageous in the face of challenges. Guide me to the right relationships and reveal the lessons in every season. Amen.

JOURNAL

CHAPTER 7

COURAGEOUS GROWTH

Taking Risks, Learning Through Failure, and Rising stronger

WHEN RISK BUILDS CONFIDENCE

Leadership isn't about being fearless—it's about showing up anyway. It's raising your hand while your heart races. It's stepping forward when you're unsure, trusting that you're called to something greater.

As an introvert, competing in pageants was daunting. The idea of standing on stage, judged by strangers, was intimidating. But I kept showing up. With each experience, I discovered more of my voice, my confidence, and my purpose.

TURNING FEEDBACK INTO FUEL

Not every pageant experience of mine ended with a crown. But each "not yet" brought something more valuable: feedback, growth, and direction. I asked questions. I studied ways to improve. And over time, I learned that a "no" doesn't mean you're not enough—it means you're not done growing.

Leadership requires humility—the kind that listens, learns, and tries again.

GROWTH COMES BEFORE THE WIN

There were times I didn't place, moments I left the stage wondering if I belonged. But I didn't give up. I asked questions. I welcomed constructive feedback. I prayed and practiced. Eventually, I *did* win some titles. Those moments weren't just markers of my achievement but of growth, discipline, and God's timing.

Winning wasn't the whole story; it was the result of showing up, growing through the process, and trusting that the hard work would pay off.

YOUR DETOUR MAY BE DIVINE

Looking back, I see that every delay, every "not yet," and every lesson was preparing me. God was cultivating something deeper—grit, grace, and unshakable confidence.

Some of your biggest breakthroughs won't come after the easiest wins. Rather, they'll come after the hardest efforts.

What feels like a detour now may actually be your divine route.

JOURNAL ACTIVITY:
WHEN HAVE YOU BEEN BRAVE?

1. Recall a time you took a risk. What made it feel uncomfortable or scary?

2. What did you learn about yourself through that experience—your values, voice, or strength?

3. Where is God inviting you to show up with more courage right now?

ACTION PLAN: STRENGTHENING
COURAGE AND CONFIDENCE

1. Identify one area where you've faced disappointment or felt like giving up.

2. Reflect on what that experience taught you about perseverance, growth, or trusting God's timing.

3. Write down one small step you can take this week to move forward with boldness, even if you're still unsure.

REFLECTION

True leaders aren't those who never fail. They're the ones who keep showing up with humility, hope, and heart. Growth happens when you keep saying yes, even after setbacks.

TAKEAWAY

Courage grows through action. Every time you rise after a fall, you build trust in yourself and in the purpose God has placed within you.

PRAYER

Lord, thank You for the lessons wrapped in disappointment. Teach me to be brave, even when I feel unsure. Remind me that I don't need to be perfect to be powerful—just need to trust You and take the next step. Amen.

JOURNAL

CHAPTER 8

BUILDING DEPTH BEFORE CLIMBING HIGHER

Sometimes leadership isn't about climbing higher—it's about stepping back with intention to grow stronger.

I stepped into leadership early—within a year of graduating nursing school. I was recruited for a formal leadership role based on the skills I'd already demonstrated. It was a significant opportunity, and I was grateful. But as I gained experience, I realized I wanted to master the clinical side of nursing. I didn't want to just hold a title—I wanted to be *excellent*. I wanted to sharpen my hands-on skills and truly understand the daily experiences of my team.

So, after a few years, I made the intentional decision to step away from formal leadership and focus on growth.

I returned to bedside nursing, working in labor and delivery, postpartum care, and the newborn nursery at a safety-net hospital—facilities serving those with few other options. Those years were humbling and deeply formative.

I didn't stop there. While gaining my clinical experience, I also enrolled in graduate courses—working toward my master's degree and a certificate in midwifery. I wanted to deepen my understanding of care, expand my leadership capacity, and build a lasting foundation.

That season taught me that leadership isn't just about moving up. It's about growing roots.

Real leadership is built from the inside out—through integrity, humility, and a commitment to the unseen work that prepares you for the next level.

ANSWERING THE CALL TO LEAD WITH BOLD CONVICTION

Growing up, I saw that not every community had equal opportunities. This shaped my view of leadership—not as a pursuit of titles or recognition, but as a commitment to uplift others, offer hope, and challenge injustice.

I was blessed with role models who embodied this. My grandmother, aunt, and cousins were nurses—strong, courageous women who not only cared for the sick but advocated for them. Some were entrepreneurs, creating opportunities through their businesses. Their example planted a seed inside of me: nursing wasn't just a career. It was a *calling*.

In high school, through the Medical Explorers program, I shadowed an operating room nurse. Her ability to empower patients and lead with quiet strength and bold compassion confirmed what I already knew in my heart: *I was called to nursing*. I didn't choose nursing simply to treat illness but to become a change agent—someone who could bridge the gap between what people needed and what the system often failed to provide.

Later, working in hospitals, I witnessed how deeply health was shaped by factors like housing, food access, and education. These weren't just "social issues." They were life-and-death realities for my patients. And leadership, I realized, meant confronting these root causes, not just treating symptoms.

No matter your field, true leadership calls you to dig deeper. Listen intently. Stand for what's right, even when it's difficult.

Every step I took away from the spotlight shaped me into the leader I prayed to become—one with vision, compassion, and a commitment to improving systems for everyone.

JOURNAL ACTIVITY:
STRENGTHENING THE FOUNDATION

1. Have you ever chosen to slow down, switch directions, or step away from something to focus on new growth? What did that season teach you about yourself?

2. What areas do you want to deepen before moving forward (e.g., skills, character, confidence, knowledge)?

3. How can you reframe "slowing down" as an investment in your future?

_____

_____

_____

_____

_____

_____

_____

ACTION PLAN: GROW BEFORE YOU GO

1. Identify a Growth Area

Choose one skill or habit that will strengthen your leadership foundation (e.g., communication, organization, empathy).

2. Take a Small Step

Find one way to begin growing in that area this week—read an article, practice a skill, or seek feedback.

3. Plan for the Long Game

Write down one long-term goal that may take time but will yield lasting impact—and commit to starting now.

TAKEAWAY

Leadership doesn't always follow a straight path. Some of the most important growth happens when you step back, shift direction, or invest in deeper learning. Every pivot is a chance to gain wisdom, serve with heart, and become the leader you're called to be.

PRAYER

God, thank You for guiding my path, even when it unfolds differently than I expect. Help me recognize growth in every season and trust that each step prepares me for greater impact. Remind me that no experience is wasted when I walk with You. Amen.

JOURNAL

CHAPTER 9

LEADING UNDER PRESSURE

Sometimes leadership means stepping up when everything feels uncertain. Resources are limited. Emotions are high. The future isn't clear. Yet, you're still called to lead.

That's what I faced when I was invited to lead several departments at a hospital specializing in high-risk pregnancies and critically ill newborns. It felt like joining a high-stakes mission team, where every decision carried weight, and every moment could change a life.

I was entrusted with overseeing departments like labor and delivery, neonatal intensive care, and pediatrics. But there was a problem. The hospital faced financial strain, budgets were tight, staffing was stretched, and the team was exhausted. Still, we had to persevere—families were counting on us.

Even in the chaos, I kept my focus on what mattered most: delivering exceptional care with dignity, respect, and compassion.

One of the most rewarding moments was helping our hospital maintain its accreditation as a Perinatal Referral Center—a trusted center for moms and babies who needed extra medical support. This recognition ensured that local families with high-risk pregnancies could access specialized care without traveling far. Our team's efforts made that possible.

WHAT I LEARNED

This season of leadership didn't just test my skills—it sharpened my voice, clarity, and courage. I learned to:

- **Lead effectively under intense pressure**

- **Make decisions that protect people**

- **Communicate clearly in uncertain moments**

- **Show up with strength, even when the path is challenging**

Leadership in difficult times isn't about pretending to be fearless. It's about showing up **with purpose**, even when the outcome isn't certain.

JOURNAL ACTIVITY:
LEADERSHIP IN TOUGH TIMES

1. Recall a time you faced a challenge—at school, work, or in your personal life. What helped you push through?

_____

_____

_____

_____

_____

2. When life feels overwhelming, what values or beliefs keep you grounded?

_____

_____

_____

_____

3. Who in your life models steady leadership? What traits do they exhibit that inspire you?

_____

_____

_____

_____

_____

_____

_____

ACTION PLAN: STAYING GROUNDED WHEN THINGS GET TOUGH

- **Create a Mission Statement:** Write one to two sentences about the kind of leader you want to be, especially in hard times.

- **Practice a Hard Decision:** What's one decision you've been avoiding? This week, take one small action toward resolving it.

- **Build Your Strength Strategy:** List three ways you recharge when life feels heavy (e.g., listening to music, praying, journaling, taking a walk).

REFLECTION

Pressure doesn't signal failure—it signals growth.

No matter your age or stage, leadership is about staying anchored in what matters most. When challenges arise, ask yourself: Am I leading from fear or from purpose? Even when things feel shaky, you can lead with clarity by staying true to who you are and what you stand for.

TAKEAWAY

Leadership isn't about having all the answers—it's about showing up, doing the right thing, and staying rooted in purpose during tough times. You don't need to be perfect. You just need to be *present*.

PRAYER

God, thank You for being with me in every challenge. When I feel overwhelmed, remind me that You've called me to lead with courage and compassion. Grant me clarity in confusion and the wisdom to act with love and strength. Amen.

JOURNAL

CHAPTER 10

WHEN MISSION CALLS YOU FORWARD

There may come times when your path shifts—not because you've failed, but because you're being called to something greater. Leading with purpose doesn't always mean climbing higher. Sometimes it means stepping into spaces that align more deeply with your mission.

Early in my career, I was entrusted with leading Women's and Children's Services at a hospital. My role involved growing programs for moms and babies, supporting doctors and nurses, and managing operations—from hiring to budgets to patient care.

Even though I was no longer in scrubs, I was still serving. Just in a different way.

But over time, I felt a pull toward something different. I wanted to be closer to the community. So, I made a bold decision: I left that hospital role and stepped into a new role at a local health department, where I helped run public health clinics serving people directly in their neighborhoods.

It wasn't a step down—it was a step toward work that felt more meaningful.

In that role, I focused on health equity[3]—making sure people had access to care, regardless of background or circumstances. It lit a new fire within me.

---

3. Health equity means making sure everyone has a fair and just opportunity to be as healthy as possible. It involves removing obstacles like poverty, discrimination, and lack of access to good jobs, education, or healthcare. **Reference:** Robert Wood Johnson Foundation (RWJF). (2023). *What is health equity?*

That spark deepened a passion I had already begun cultivating. In 2016, I launched a nonprofit. The mission? To support students from all walks of life—especially those underrepresented in healthcare, public health, or STEM careers. Through scholarships and mentorship, we're building a more diverse, compassionate future, one student at a time.

JOURNAL ACTIVITY:
MAPPING YOUR PASSION TO PURPOSE

1. Passion Check-In

What issues or communities are you most passionate about serving? Why do they matter to you?

_____

_____

_____

_____

_____

2. Your Strengths in Action

What leadership skills—such as listening, planning, or encouraging others—do you already have that could make a difference now?

_____

_____

_____

_____

_____

3. When Purpose Meets Change

Think about a time when life changed directions. What doors opened? What did you learn about yourself?

_____

_____

_____

_____

_____

ACTION PLAN: LIVING YOUR MISSION WHEREVER YOU ARE

- **Step 1:** Choose one issue or cause that matters deeply to you.

- **Step 2:** Find a way to get involved—through online platforms, in school, or in your community.

- **Step 3:** Take one action this month, such as joining a group, mentoring, or raising awareness.

Purpose isn't about changing the entire world. It's about showing up with heart wherever you are.

REFLECTION

You don't have to stay in one lane to grow as a leader. Your path may twist, turn, or even loop back—but each step shapes the leader you're becoming. Whether you're leading in a classroom, clinic, or a community center, what matters is how you show up.

Leadership is more than a title—it's living your purpose. Ask yourself, "Why am I here?" and have the courage to follow the answer.

TAKEAWAY

Leadership is less about climbing a ladder and more about answering a call. Sometimes, the most meaningful shifts come when you prioritize *purpose* over *position*.

PRAYER

God, thank You for reminding me that leadership doesn't always follow a straight path. Help me to lead with purpose in every place You call me. Whether seen or unseen, may I serve with heart, grow with humility, and stay aligned with the mission You've placed on my life. Amen.

JOURNAL

CHAPTER 11

EXPANDING YOUR INFLUENCE

WHEN NEW SPACES CALL YOU FORWARD

For much of my career, I worked in healthcare—hospitals, clinics, home health, and public health—where I could directly see the impact of my work on patients, families, and communities. But over time, I felt a quiet nudge. While I remained passionate about health equity and access, I sensed my next step would stretch beyond the walls of traditional care settings. I felt called to reach more people in new ways.

That nudge became a calling.

Just before the COVID-19 pandemic, a recruiter approached me to lead the development of national health science career pathways for a major education technology company. This company served thousands of K–12 students through online and blended learning, many from rural, low-income, or nontraditional backgrounds.

It was a big shift. I traded scrubs, stethoscopes, and hospital boardrooms for the unfamiliar world of virtual learning and digital platforms. I didn't have all the answers. But I brought something powerful: a unique skill set shaped by years of nursing leadership, lived experience, deep values, and an unwavering belief in the potential of young people when equipped with the right tools.

BEING THE ONLY—AND STILL BELONGING

As the company's only nurse leader, I brought a perspective no one else could. I saw both the gaps and the possibilities. I worked to build strong health science programs, develop partnerships with colleges and employers, and create pathways into careers in nursing, public health, and healthcare for students across nearly forty states and beyond.

Eventually, I was entrusted with a broader role—overseeing career programming, work-based learning, and industry partnerships. Through that work, I supported more than 60,000 students, many from diverse socioeconomic backgrounds.

My work no longer took place in a hospital, but I was still leading, advocating, and opening doors.

Being "the only" in a space isn't always easy, but it's deeply meaningful. Your voice carries unique weight. Your presence fills a gap. Your perspective sparks possibilities. Sometimes, stepping into new or unfamiliar spaces is an act of leadership in itself.

WHEN YOU BRING WHAT'S MISSING, YOU SPARK WHAT'S POSSIBLE

One of the reasons I was drawn to this role was because the company saw innovation differently. They welcomed people with new perspectives—those who didn't come from the conventional backgrounds. People like me.

Because I was a trained nurse, I approached challenges with a different mindset. Nurses are taught to assess, adapt, communicate, and advocate. We look beyond the surface to care for the whole person, not just what's visible in the moment. We notice what's missing, what's possible, and what needs to change.

That training became one of my greatest assets in this new space.

I didn't need to fit someone else's mold. I was hired to reshape it—to build new programs, create innovative ideas, and expand what was possible for students everywhere.

Innovation isn't just about technology or having the loudest ideas in the room. Sometimes, it's about offering a different lens—seeing overlooked challenges and offering solutions rooted in compassion, experience, and vision.

When you bring your full self—your background, faith, and quiet wisdom—you create space for new growth. Something transformational.

JOURNAL ACTIVITY:
EXPANDING YOUR LEADERSHIP REACH

1. What new spaces might need your leadership, even if they feel unfamiliar?

Write down one area or industry you're curious about and how your current strengths could serve it.

_____

_____

_____

_____

_____

2. What fear might be holding you back from your next opportunity?

Imagine facing it with faith and preparation. What would that look like?

_____

_____

_____

_____

_____

3. Who believes in your potential, even when you don't see it?

Write them a note of gratitude or share your next goal with them for encouragement.

ACTION PLAN: LEADING BEYOND LIMITS

- **Identify a New Arena:** Name one space outside of your current environment where your leadership could make an impact (e.g., schools, community organizations, online platforms).

- **Name a Fear and a First Step:** Choose a fear that's been holding you back. Identify one small, tangible step to confront it this month.

- **Prepare to Pivot:** Explore a webinar, course, or mentorship opportunity to grow in a new direction, even if it feels uncomfortable at first.

REFLECTION

Leadership isn't always about titles or corner offices—it's about showing up in unfamiliar spaces that need your voice. It's stepping out of the known and into the possible. God often grows our influence in places where we feel least prepared, not to overwhelm us, but to remind us that our power comes from Him.

If you sense a shift or crave something more, don't be afraid to explore. Trust that your gifts can stretch across industries, spaces, and communities—your impact was never meant to be confined to one lane.

TAKEAWAY

Leadership isn't always linear. Your next assignment may lead you into unfamiliar territory, but that's where growth thrives. Say "yes" to the opportunities that stretch you, even if—no, *especially* if—they scare you.

PRAYER

God, thank You for calling me to lead, even in unfamiliar places. When fear or uncertainty arises, remind me that You are with me and You equip me for every open door. Help me to lead with courage, humility, and purpose, wherever You place me. Amen.

JOURNAL

CHAPTER 12

THE POWER OF MENTORSHIP AND SPONSORSHIP

FINDING YOUR CIRCLE OF SUPPORT

At every stage of my journey, I've been guided by a circle of supporters—mentors who invested in my growth and sponsors who elevated my name in rooms I hadn't yet entered. These people formed what I now call my "personal board of directors." They each played different roles, but all helped shape the leader I am today.

Understanding the difference between a mentor and a sponsor is key:

- **A mentor** walks beside you—offering advice, encouragement, and a safe place to grow.

- **A sponsor** speaks on your behalf—using their influence to create opportunities you may not have access to on your own.

You don't need a title to be a mentor or sponsor. You just need to be intentional about showing up for others.

WHEN SOMEONE BELIEVES IN YOU–AND BACKS YOU

In one of my early leadership roles, I had a supervisor who didn't just mentor me—she sponsored me. She saw potential in me and chose to invest in my development. She gave me high-visibility assignments, helped me find my voice, and ensured I had a seat at decision-making tables. One of those assignments changed the trajectory of my career.

I was asked to launch a brand-new service for pregnant women with high-risk pregnancies. It was an innovative model that involved telephonic outreach by nurses—leveraging electronic medical records to identify women early, coordinate their care, and ensure they received the support needed for a healthy delivery. This work mattered deeply. And because my sponsor trusted me—and removed barriers when I needed help—I was able to lead with confidence, supported by a stellar team of nurses and physicians.

That service is still active today, more than ten years later, and has supported thousands of women and babies in the region. It wasn't just a professional win. It was a reminder that the right sponsor can unlock both purpose and possibility in powerful ways.

LIFTING AS YOU CLIMB

Mentors have helped me gain clarity and confidence. Sponsors have opened doors. Now, I make it my mission to do the same for others.

Whether it's answering a student's message, writing a recommendation letter, or advocating for someone's opportunity—I believe in *lifting as I climb*.

You can be that person too. You don't need to have it all figured out. Just be willing to notice others, believe in them, and help them rise.

REFLECTION

Think about someone who saw your potential before you fully did. Maybe it was a teacher, coach, employer, or even a friend. Their encouragement lit a fire within you—and that's what mentors and sponsors do. They offer more than advice; they offer belief.

TAKEAWAY

Mentorship and sponsorship aren't just helpful—they're essential. You were never meant to walk your leadership journey alone. The right people can help you unlock your next level. And when it's your turn, be that person for someone else.

JOURNAL ACTIVITY:
MENTORS, SPONSORS, AND YOU

1. Who's in Your Corner?

List one or two people who have guided or supported you in your personal or leadership journey. What impact have they had on your growth?

2. Sponsor vs. Mentor

Have you experienced both types of support? How were they different, and why did each matter?

3. Be the Support

Identify someone in your circle (a sibling, classmate, or coworker) who could benefit from your encouragement or advocacy. What's one thing you can do this week to support their growth?

ACTION PLAN: BUILDING AND BECOMING

- **Reach Out:** Send a note of thanks to a mentor or sponsor. Let them know the difference they made.

- **Give Back:** Offer help or guidance to someone newer on the path.

- **Be Intentional:** Set a goal to mentor one person this year or advocate for someone deserving of recognition.

PRAYER

Dear God, thank You for the people who have walked with me, encouraged me, and spoken life into my potential. Help me to be that same light for others—to offer wisdom, support, and advocacy to those still finding their way. Remind me that leadership is not just about rising—but about lifting others as I go. Amen.

JOURNAL

CHAPTER 13

A LIFELONG COMMITMENT TO GROWTH AND LEADERSHIP

There's a myth that learning stops once you land a job or graduate. But real leadership thrives on continuous growth—and that growth never expires.

After years in healthcare and public health, I felt a pull to keep learning and expand my influence. So, I stepped into a new opportunity: I became an Education Policy Fellow.

A fellowship, in this context, is a special learning and leadership experience—kind of like a deep dive into a new subject or system. As a Fellow, I explored how policy decisions shape high schools, colleges, and career programs. My goal was to understand the bigger picture and advocate for change, especially for students often overlooked.

Around the same time, I stayed active in my professional community. I was elected Board President of a statewide nursing association, representing over 120,000 nurses. It was a big role, but the mission—advocating for better staffing, fair policies, and healthier workplaces for nurses—kept me grounded.

These roles weren't about collecting titles. They were about growing in purpose and expanding impact. And they reminded me of a vital truth: *leadership is a lifelong journey.*

JOURNAL ACTIVITY:
WHAT DOES GROWTH LOOK LIKE FOR YOU?

1. What area of your life or leadership do you want to grow in right now?

_____

_____

_____

_____

_____

_____

2. What learning opportunities—formal or informal—could help you achieve that growth?

_____

_____

_____

_____

_____

_____

3. Who inspires you to keep growing, and why?

ACTION PLAN: START SMALL, DREAM BIG

- Choose one podcast, article, or book this month to stretch your perspective.

- Set one professional or personal development goal for the next six months.

- Join a leadership club, youth board, or professional group to learn from others.

REFLECTION

"Enlarge your house; build an addition.

Spread out your home, and spare no expense!

For you will soon be bursting at the seams…" (Isaiah 54:2–3, nlt)

God often prepares us for greater things before we even realize it. But preparation requires a willingness to grow into the spaces He's creating for you.

TAKEAWAY

Leadership doesn't require a title. It requires growth, courage, and obedience. Your next level of leadership may not look like anyone else's—but if you stay curious, humble, and open to learning, you'll be ready when the door opens.

PRAYER

God, thank You for every step of my journey—even the hard ones. Give me the discipline to keep learning, the wisdom to grow, and the boldness to lead with love and purpose. Amen.

JOURNAL

CHAPTER 14

FAITH-FILLED WINS AND FULL-CIRCLE MOMENTS

sat in my office, refreshing my email, when I saw the message. My heart skipped a beat as I read:

We are pleased to inform you of your selection for Fellowship in the American Academy of Nursing...

I dropped to my knees, then lay prostrate on the floor, tears streaming down my face as I praised the Lord. This wasn't just a professional win; it was a spiritual breakthrough. A rainbow piercing through a storm.

This recognition arrived during one of the darkest and most challenging seasons of my life. I had been pressing forward—working, leading, and serving—while carrying burdens few knew about. Yet here was God, shining His light in a way only He could. His presence was palpable, as if He whispered, "I see you. I've been with you all along."

But let me be clear: the journey to this moment wasn't easy.

The previous year, I applied and didn't get accepted. I was disappointed. I questioned whether I belonged in such spaces. But instead of giving up, I applied again. And this time, I was selected—not only as a Fellow but as part of the Academy's 50th Anniversary Class.

The honor held even deeper meaning because of the lack of representation. Historically, few nurses of color have been recognized at this level. I felt seen. Validated. Humbled. And ready to do more—not for applause, but for impact.

To put this in perspective: being named a Fellow of the American Academy of Nursing is akin to an actor winning an Oscar. It's one of the highest honors in the profession, with a rigorous nomination and review process reserved for those who've made extraordinary contributions to health on a local, national, or global scale.

There are more than 29 million nurses around the world[4] and about 4.3 million of us in the United States.[5] Of all nurses, just over 3200 have earned this recognition. That places me in less than 0.1% of nurses nationally—and in an even smaller group globally.

I don't share that for praise—I share it to show what's possible. I share it for every young person who's ever doubted their place in the room. I share it because moments like this are built on prayer, perseverance, and purpose.

4. World Health Organization. (2022, March 29). *Nursing and midwifery*

5. Health Resources and Services Administration, Bureau of Health Workforce. (2024). *Nurse survey fact sheet 2024* [Fact sheet]. U.S. Department of Health and Human Services.

JOURNAL ACTIVITY:
REFLECT ON A WIN (BIG OR SMALL)

1. What's a recent accomplishment you're proud of?

_____

_____

_____

_____

_____

2. What did you learn about yourself through that process?

_____

_____

_____

_____

_____

3. Who helped you get there, and how can you thank or encourage them?

ACTION PLAN: SHINE WITHOUT APOLOGY

- List three ways you can share your work or passion more openly (e.g., writing, speaking, mentoring).

- Identify one space (virtual or in-person) where your story could inspire others.

- Ask a trusted friend or mentor for feedback on how you "show up" as a leader.

REFLECTION

"For we are God's handiwork, created in Christ Jesus to do good works, which God prepared in advance for us to do." (Ephesians 2:10, NIV)

You are not an accident. Your work has purpose. Your impact matters. Even when you feel unseen, God is writing a powerful story through your life.

TAKEAWAY

Victory is not about fame—it's about *faithfulness*. The applause is temporary, but the lives you touch are eternal. Celebrate your wins, honor the journey, and never stop giving God the glory.

PRAYER

Lord, thank You for every door You've opened and every lesson You've taught me along the way. Help me celebrate the wins—not with pride, but with praise. May every victory reflect Your grace. Amen.

JOURNAL

CHAPTER 15

EMBRACING WHAT MAKES YOU DIFFERENT

Some of history's greatest changemakers—Jesus Christ, Dr. Martin Luther King Jr., and Mahatma Gandhi—were misunderstood in their time. While I don't compare myself to these extraordinary figures, their stories teach us something important: being different isn't a flaw. It's often your greatest strength.

Growing up, I always felt a little bit... *different*. My parents often spoke words of affirmation over me, saying, "You were destined for greatness." But as a child, I didn't want to be different—I wanted to blend in. I longed to be like everyone else, yet I always felt like a square peg in a round hole.

I remember being five years old, sitting at my babysitter's house while other kids watched cartoons, laughing and clapping along. I sat quietly, thinking, *I really don't want to watch this.* Even then, I sensed I saw the world differently.

In school, I had a few close friends—but because I was quiet, I was often misunderstood as "stuck up." The truth? I was an observer. I preferred to think before speaking.

Later, my pastor described me as "peculiar" during a sermon. Initially, I didn't know how to take it. Then he added, "God's people are often peculiar." That moment reframed how I viewed myself—I wasn't too quiet or too different. I was uniquely created, with purpose.

LETTING MY WORK SPEAK

As I entered leadership spaces, I realized that your voice matters, even if it doesn't sound like everyone else's.

In many rooms, I was the only Black woman—or one of few. I'd share ideas in meetings, only to see them ignored ... until someone else repeated them and received credit. I later learned these were *microaggressions*—subtle ways of saying, "Your voice doesn't count here."

So, I got strategic.

I let my work speak.

Early in my career, I tackled tough projects—ones others passed on:

- √ A home care agency at risk of losing its license unless major changes were made

- √ A hospital unit on the verge of shutting down, serving moms and babies in need

- √ A system slowing things down and keeping patients from getting timely help

- √ New programs that didn't yet exist, needing to be built from scratch

None of these assignments were glamorous. But they mattered. And they required more than just technical skills. They called for:

- **Strategic thinking:** Solving big problems with a long-term plan

- **Emotional intelligence:** understanding people's emotions and needs

- **Courage and patience:** tackling hard things, even when it's slow or unclear

- **Business sense:** making smart, ethical decisions with limited resources had

- **Prayer and perseverance**: leaning on faith and staying the course

This was intentional, values-based leadership—the kind that doesn't always seek the spotlight but creates meaningful, lasting change.

Eventually, I became the first nurse in my region to earn a doctorate at a national company that had teams across the country. That opened new doors to rooms where policies were shaped and lives were impacted. It wasn't about being the loudest. It was about being a consistent, trusted leader who showed up with purpose.

FINDING MY OWN VOICE

Over time, I realized I didn't need to change who I was—I needed to use what I already had.

I began speaking on panels, writing articles, mentoring younger professionals, and accepting invitations to appear on TV and at conferences, even when I was nervous. Every time I showed up authentically, I saw the difference my voice could make.

God doesn't require you to be the loudest—He just calls you to be faithful.

If you feel unseen or unheard, don't shrink back. Let your work, gifts, and integrity speak.

And when it's time, your voice will break through.

JOURNAL ACTIVITY: FINDING YOUR VOICE

1. What sometimes makes it hard for you to speak up?

2. What message or passion is worth sharing, even if your voice shakes?

3. What are three ways you can "speak" without using words (e.g., through action, writing, or creativity)?

4. Recall a time when your quiet strength made an impact. What happened?

ACTION PLAN: USE WHAT YOU'VE GOT

- Identify one talent or strength you can use to amplify a message that matters to you.

- Start or join a group focused on a cause that aligns with your values.

- Practice a "confidence pitch"—a one-sentence introduction of yourself and your passion.

- Find a mentor who can help you grow more confident in your voice.

REFLECTION

"A gift opens the way and ushers the giver into the presence of the great." (Proverbs 18:16 NIV)

"Whether you turn to the right or to the left, your ears will hear a voice behind you saying, 'This is the way; walk in it.'" (Isaiah 30:21, NIV)

These verses remind us that God uses what's already within us. When we trust Him and stay rooted in purpose, our gifts will make room for us, even in spaces where we once felt invisible.

TAKEAWAY

You don't need to be the loudest person in the room to make an impact. You just have to show up, speak with courage, and trust that your voice—however quiet—is powerful when guided by purpose.

JOURNAL

CHAPTER 16

LEADING WITH INTEGRITY AND INNER STRENGTH

DOING WHAT'S RIGHT, EVEN WHEN IT'S HARD

Leadership doesn't always demand grand speeches. Sometimes, it's about doing what's right—especially when it's hard.

In one of my leadership roles, I began to hear concerns from both staff and patients. Despite our best efforts, our unit lacked enough team members to safely care for all the moms and babies. People were tired, stressed, and overstretched.

As their leader, I faced a choice:

- **Stay quiet** and try to manage with our limited resources—play it safe, stick to the approved budget, and avoid rocking the boat with senior leadership to protect my job and future in the organization.

- **Speak up**—even if it meant challenging the status quo or risking my position—to advocate for more staff and better, safer care.

I chose to speak up.

No one prompted me. I didn't wait for others to notice the problem. By listening to my team, I knew something needed to change. Leading with integrity meant standing up for what was right—even if it was uncomfortable, even when it made others uneasy, and even if it meant putting my own position on the line.

I collaborated with our finance team to gather data, comparing our hospital's patient needs with others in the region. The findings were clear: our team was caring for patients who were sicker and required more intensive care. The numbers supported our case.

With that evidence, I crafted a strong proposal and shared it with leadership. It wasn't easy. There were questions, pushback, and moments of doubt about whether change would happen. But I persisted, keeping my team updated and working alongside them to demonstrate our commitment to improving care.

Eventually, the staffing plan was approved. We added team members, improving patient safety and staff support. The unit's atmosphere improved, and people felt seen and valued again.

This experience taught me that **leading with integrity sometimes means being the first to speak up**, even when others stay quiet. It's not always popular or easy. But it's always worth it.

THE 4-POINT CHECK FOR ETHICAL LEADERSHIP

Every leader needs a way to stay grounded, especially when the path is unclear. That's why I created this simple 4-point check to guide you through tough decisions.

Each question is rooted in real leadership moments and will help you pause, reflect, and lead with integrity. Whether you're making choices at school, work, or in your community, these points will help you lead in a way that honors your values and respects others.

You can use this check-in when you're unsure what to do, feeling pressured from others, or want to make a decision that reflects who you truly are—and who you're becoming.

LEADERSHIP COMPASS FOR ETHICAL DECISION-MAKING

Based on Maslow's Hierarchy of Needs[6]

1. Check In: Start with You

Maslow Level: Physiological & Safety Needs

Ask Yourself:

- How am I feeling—physically, mentally, emotionally?

- Am I tired, overwhelmed, or drained?

- What do I need to think clearly and lead well?

Why it Matters:

Unmet basic needs can cloud judgement when leading. Self-awareness enables you to lead from a place of strength, not stress.

Reflect Before You Act:

"Before I decide, have I paused to care for myself first?"

2. Lead with Respect: See the Person First

Maslow Level: Belonging & Esteem Needs

Ask Yourself:

- Have I truly listened to everyone involved?

- Am I considering how this decision impacts those around me?

- Will this choice make others feel respected and included?

Why it Matters:

Real leadership isn't about power—it's about people. When others feel seen, heard, and valued, trust and teamwork strengthen.

Reflect Before You Act:

"Am I lifting someone up or leaving someone out?"

---

6. **Maslow's Hierarchy of Needs** is a theory in psychology developed by Abraham Maslow in 1943. It explains that people have different levels of needs—from basic ones like food and safety to deeper needs like belonging, confidence, and purpose. His theory helps explain how meeting these needs can shape our ability to grow, learn, and lead more effectively.

3. Do More Good Than Harm

Maslow Level: Esteem & Self-Actualization

Ask Yourself:

- Could this action cause harm, even unintentionally?

- Is there a better approach that honors people while still achieving results?

- Am I acting from kindness or reacting to pressure?

Why it Matters:

Good intentions matter, but so does impact. Ethical leadership involves being mindful of both.

Reflect Before You Act:

"If this decision affected me, how would I feel?"

4. Grow with Integrity: Who Am I Becoming?

Maslow Level: Self-Actualization & Transcendence

Ask Yourself:

- Does this align with my values and who I'm becoming?

- Will I be proud of this decision later?

- What does this choice say about my leadership?

Why it Matters:

Every decision shapes your character. Leading with integrity builds trust in yourself and your values.

Reflect Before You Act:

"What story will this decision reveal about me?"

ACTION PLAN: PUTTING THE
4-POINT CHECK INTO PRACTICE

1. Keep it handy

Print or save this checklist for easy reference in your phone or journal.

2. Use it in real time

When facing a tough choice—at school, work, or in relationships—walk through these four points to guide your decision.

3. Start a conversation

Share this tool with a mentor, teacher, or trusted friend. Discussing it can bring fresh clarity.

4. Reflect on results

Notice how your confidence, clarity, and outcomes shift when you lead with self-awareness, respect, integrity, and vision.

JOURNAL ACTIVITY:

1. Recall a time when you noticed something that didn't feel right. Did you speak up? Why or why not?

_____

_____

_____

_____

_____

_____

2. What does "doing the right thing" look like in your school, community, or workplace?

_____

_____

_____

_____

_____

_____

3. Have you ever stayed silent, despite feeling strongly about an issue? What held you back?

_____

_____

_____

_____

_____

_____

ACTION PLAN:

- Write down **two values** that guide your decisions. Keep them somewhere visible.

- Identify **one small way** to speak up or advocate for someone this week.

- If you're unsure how to act, discuss it with a trusted mentor, teacher, or friend.

REFLECTION

"Speak up for those who cannot speak for themselves … defend the rights of the poor and needy." (Proverbs 31:8–9, NIV)

You don't need to be in charge to lead. Leadership involves honesty, attentiveness, and using your voice—even when it's uncomfortable.

Being a change agent often means challenging the status quo and stepping forward when others stay silent. That's true leadership.

KEY INSIGHT

Leadership is doing what's right, even if you stand alone. You don't need a title to lead—just courage, faith, and a heart that cares enough to act.

PRAYER

God, grant me bravery to speak when silence is easier. Give me wisdom to discern what's right and strength to act with love and integrity. Let my actions reflect Your light and my voice bring hope, healing, and justice to those who need it most. Amen.

JOURNAL

CHAPTER 17

BOUNCING BACK WITH PURPOSE

A LESSON ON REJECTION I'LL NEVER FORGET

'll never forget something my professor said during a writing course in my doctoral program. We were learning how research papers get published and were introduced to the "peer review process." In this process, experts in the field read your work and provide feedback before it can be approved. Sometimes the feedback is helpful. Sometimes it's harsh. And yes—papers get rejected all the time.

But my professor said something that stuck with me: "Rejection isn't personal. It's part of the process."

I had never thought of rejection with that perspective before.

WHAT I'VE LEARNED ABOUT SETBACKS

That one sentence changed the way I think—not just about rejection, but about failure too. Here's what I've come to understand:

- **Rejection** often comes before something begins—a job you didn't get, a proposal that wasn't accepted.

- **Failure** happens in the midst of action—a project that didn't go as planned, or a team effort that missed the mark.

Both can sting. But both can fuel growth for you—as long as you embrace them.

GOD'S BIGGER PICTURE

I didn't always get the roles I applied for. One leadership position, in particular, stung deeply. But instead of staying discouraged, I prayed, listened, and kept growing. Years later, I was elected president of a statewide nursing association—something far beyond what I had imagined.

That's how God works. He sees the whole picture when we only glimpse the next piece.

LESSONS FROM THE JOURNEY

1. Rejection isn't a Reflection of Your Worth:

Sometimes a "no" can be protection or preparation for a greater "yes."

2. Failure Means You Had the Courage to Try:

Not every risk succeeds—but each one teaches you something.

3. Your Voice Still Matters:

Even when overlooked, keep showing up. Let your work speak.

4. God's Timing is Always Right:

Wait on Him. What's meant for you won't pass you by.

JOURNAL ACTIVITY:
REWRITING THE STORY OF REJECTION

1. Write about a time you were told "no." How did it feel, and how did you respond?

_____

_____

_____

_____

_____

_____

2. Reflect on a mistake or failure. What did it teach you?

_____

_____

_____

_____

_____

_____

3. Has a door ever closed, only for something better to open? Describe it.

4. What are you waiting or hoping for now? What might God be teaching you in this season of waiting?

ACTION PLAN:
TURNING SETBACKS INTO STRENGTH

- **Name it:** Write down one challenge, rejection, or failure that still weighs on you.

- **Reframe it:** Identify a strength or skill this experience revealed in you.

- **Move forward:** List one small, brave step you can take this week to keep going with faith and confidence.

REFLECTION

"And we know that in all things God works for the good of those who love him, who have been called according to his purpose." (Romans 8:28, NIV)

Every setback, every "no," every disappointment—God can use it all. Even when you don't understand the reason right away, trust that He's shaping your story for good.

TAKEAWAY

Setbacks don't define you. They *refine* you. Leadership isn't about perfection; it's about staying faithful, learning as you go, and trusting that God's plan is bigger than any temporary "no."

PRAYER

Lord, thank You for every closed door and every hard moment that draws me closer to You. When I feel discouraged or rejected, remind me that You are still at work in my life. Help me grow from every setback and trust that nothing is wasted in Your hands. Amen.

JOURNAL

CHAPTER 18

YOUR NEXT CHAPTER STARTS HERE

You've journeyed through this book—reflecting, journaling, and maybe even uncovering new truths about yourself along the way. Now what?

This final chapter isn't just a recap. It's a call to action. A charge. A moment to pause, breathe, and declare, "I'm ready."

WHAT WE'VE LEARNED TOGETHER

Here's a quick recap of the leadership strategies you now have in your toolkit:

10 Leadership Lessons to Carry Forward

- **Purposeful Pivots Build Strength:**

    Your path may twist and turn. Growth often happens in the shift, not the spotlight.

- **Faith in the Process:**

    Trust God's timing. Delays don't always signal denial—they're often *preparation*.

- **Speak Up with Courage:**

  Advocacy matters. Use your voice to stand for what's right, even when it feels uncomfortable.

- **Mentorship and Sponsorship Are Game-Changers:**

  Walk with those who guide you. Learn to open doors for others too.

- **Rejection Is Redirection:**

  A "no" may simply mean "not this time." Keep growing and stay ready.

- **Lead with Integrity:**

  Do the right thing, even when it's inconvenient, unpopular, or unnoticed.

- **Shine Without Apology:**

  You are not an accident. Your work has purpose. Your impact matters.

- **Let Your Voice Make Impact:**

  Whether through writing, building, leading, or showing up, your voice makes room for you.

- **Rest Is Part of Leadership:**

  Real leadership isn't about power—it's about people

- **This Is Only the Beginning:**

  You're not behind—you're *becoming*. The world needs your unique contribution.

ACTION PLAN: LIVING WHAT YOU'VE LEARNED

1. Pick one lesson that hit home for you.

Write it where you'll see often.

2. Create a personal leadership vision statement.

(Just two to three lines about the leader you aspire to be.)

3. Share this book with someone who needs it.

Leadership thrives in community.

PRAYER

Dear Lord, thank You for walking with me through this journey. Help me apply what I've learned and lead with grace, humility, and purpose. Show me where You want me to go next and give me courage to follow. I trust You to guide my path, equip me with wisdom, and open doors no one can shut. Amen.

JOURNAL

INTERVIEW WITH FUTURE ME

Sometimes the clearest way to know where you're headed is to picture the version of yourself already living it. Think of this as a chance to sit down with your future self—the one who's faced challenges, made bold choices, and trusted God every step of the way.

Let this moment be both a prayer and a declaration. Dream big. Be specific. And be honest. You're not just writing answers—you're *planting seeds*.

1. Where are you living or working in the future? What does your environment look and feel like?

_____

_____

_____

_____

_____

2. What kind of leader have you become? How do people describe you?

3. What are you doing that brings you purpose and joy?

4. What's something you're proud of—something only you and God know how hard it was to achieve?

5. What lessons did you learn the hard way? What would you do differently now?

6. Who helped you along the way? How did you thank them or pay it forward?

7. What advice would you give your younger self who's still figuring it all out?

8. How has your faith grown since today? What role does God play in your life now?

Signature of Future Me:

Date:

"God's not done with me yet.
And I'm becoming the leader I was created to be."